JOURNEYS INTO BEDFORDSHIRE

This book of ink drawings reveals an intriguing historic heritage, and captures the spirit of England's rural heartland, ranging widely over cottages and stately homes, over bridges, churches and mills, over sandy woods, chalk downs and watery river valleys.

Every corner of Bedfordshire has been explored in the search for material, and, although the choice of subjects is essentially a personal one, the resulting collection represents a unique record of the environment today.

The notes and maps which accompany the drawings lend depth to the book, and will assist others in their own journeys around this fascinating county.

'Anthony Mackay's pen-and-ink drawings are of outstanding quality. An architectural graduate, he is equally at home depicting landscapes and buildings. The medium he uses is, in a master's hands, better able to show both depth and detail than any photograph and I have rarely seen the equal of the drawings that grace this book.'

Bedfordshire Life

The author and artist was born in Cheshire in 1937 and graduated in architecture from the University of Liverpool in 1961. He has designed buildings in Denmark, Greece, the Middle East, Germany and Britain, and practises in Bedford.

His extensive travels in Europe, the United States and India have resulted in paintings, pastels and ink drawings, many of which have been exhibited publicly and been bought for private collections.

A companion volume, Journeys into Hertfordshire, with a foreword by the Marquess of Salisbury from Hatfield House, was published in October, 1991.

A third collection, Journeys into Oxfordshire, with a foreword by the Duke of Marlborough from Blenheim Palace, appeared in October 1993.

JOURNEYS INTO BEDFORDSHIRE

A COLLECTION OF
INK DRAWINGS

ANTHONY MACKAY

FOREWORD BY
THE MARQUESS OF TAVISTOCK

This pocket edition first published November 1994

Original edition first published September 1987
Reprinted October 1988

The Book Castle
12 Church Street
Dunstable
Bedfordshire LU5 4RU

ISBN 1 871199 17 4

Printed and bound by the
Alden Press, Oxford

Front Cover: Oak Cottage, Church End, Ravensden
Back cover: Priory Church of St. Peter, Dunstable

CONTENTS

OVER THE LAW COURTS, BEDFORD

To Elaine

FOREWORD
by
THE MARQUESS OF TAVISTOCK

Woburn Abbey, Woburn, Bedfordshire MK43 0TP · Woburn 666 · Telex 826621

I am delighted to write this Foreword, as Anthony Mackay has produced a unique collection of ink drawings devoted to the landscape and buildings of Bedfordshire.

It is the result of three years of sketching, photography and historical studies, and represents an important record of our environment in the 1980s.

The drawings reflect the fact that, despite proximity to London, and the pressures for development imposed ·by this, Bedfordshire remains essentially rural in character. Our county gives people an intimate and often beautiful patchwork of farmlands, wooded hills and river valleys, countless intriguing buildings and distinctive relics of the past.

Primarily a book of favourite places, it will encourage others to go out and explore their county.

Marquess of Tavistock

ACKNOWLEDGEMENTS

For permission to make drawings and to use them in this volume, I would like to thank the following individuals and institutions, who kindly allowed me onto their land and gave me invaluable help in compiling information about their buildings:

Miss H. and Mr W. Battcock of Witts End Close, Eversholt
Bedfordshire County Council
Bedford Museum
Mr Diamond of Bushmead House
Mr and Mrs Dorman of Houghton Conquest
Miss Davies of Pirton Grange
English Heritage
Mr and Mrs Fairweather of Campton Manor
The Moathouse Hotel, Bedford
Mr Mark Mackay of Pavenham

North Bedfordshire Borough Council
The National Trust
Mrs Orlebar of Hinwick House
The RSPB of Sandy
The RAF and USAF of Chicksands
The Marquess and Marchioness of Tavistock
Mr and Mrs J. Struthers of Astwick Bury Farm
Mr Samuel Whitbread of Southill Park
Mr P. C. Woodcraft of Church End, Ravensden
Mr N. Wilde of Bedford Central Library

In addition I would like to acknowledge the unwitting role played by craftsmen, farmers, builders and artists, without whose work over preceding centuries we would not have the material to stimulate such a book.

For their advice and support during the four years of work I wish to thank Roy Barton, Brian Jarvis, David Potter and Betty Chambers.

OUSE REFLECTIONS

INTRODUCTION

Within the small county of Bedfordshire all the essential elements of rural England are condensed into one rich and varied landscape.

The fields and hedgerows carpeting the gently undulating valleys, give way to the bare chalk uplands of the Chilterns along the southern boundary, to the intimate wooded hillocks and ridges of the Greensand in the centre, and in the north, to the languorous course of the River Ouse, as it leaves the Midlands for the Fens.

It is a land of detail rather than grand gesture. To the casual eye the county might seem very ordinary, but the real Bedfordshire only emerges from close study. Because it lacks the major drama of mountainous or coastal areas, it requires exploration beyond the broad view, and examination of the intricacies of the landscape and the substance of buildings and structures within it.

It is here that the beauties of Bedfordshire are to be found.

Virtually unscathed by industrial blight, and with only limited urban presence, the countryside remains unspoilt, and has the character and atmosphere of a backwater. This is its great strength, allowing the survival of nature and buildings in a region lying within the orbit of London.

My journeys into Bedfordshire between 1983 and 1986, and the resulting drawings, are the subject of this book. Every town and village has been visited to find worthwhile buildings and features.

Footpaths and bridleways enabled me to reach the more remote downlands, where remnants of prehistoric settlements could be seen, and the line of the ancient Icknield Way could be followed.

The low hills at Sundon and Sharpenhoe, where the chalk slopes are steep on their north face, give the impression of height and provide long open views across the valleys below.

In the sandy heathland stretching from Woburn and Aspley Guise in the west, to the ridge at Sandy in the east, are some of the most inviting tracts of countryside imaginable, the woodlands enriched by a great variety of tree species, and teeming with plant and wildlife.

Probably the finest natural feature is the River Ouse, which crosses the northern half of the county in a series of meandering loops before reaching Bedford, and then widens as it flows eastwards into Cambridgeshire. The string of limestone villages between Turvey and Bromham are linked by the river, resulting in the building of many elegant stone bridges, and several imposing, but now disused, watermills.

The greater part of the county, however, is made up of rolling farmland, of fields and woods woven together by an elaborate web of hedges, lanes and pathways. This is the essence of Bedfordshire, and it is here that the richest seam of architecture is to be found, and where most of the illustrations in this book are concentrated.

The varied geology of the county has produced the limestone villages of the Ouse valley, the red clay brick buildings of the Bedford and Marston Vale, the white clunch-stone churches of the chalk bands, and the timber-framed thatched cottages of the wooded river plains in the east.

It is remarkable to find such diversity packed into such a small area of the country, and this is what makes it so fascinating to explore.

HOCKLIFFE LANDSCAPE

STEVINGTON VILLAGE CROSS

Amongst the outstanding individual features of Bedfordshire are: the country houses at Wrest Park, Southill, Hinwick, Luton Hoo, and Woburn Abbey; the churches of Felmersham and Dunstable; the manor houses of Meppershall, Campton, and Pertenhall; the villages of Swineshead, Old Warden, Woburn, and Stevington; the parks at Odell, Stockgrove, and Whipsnade; and the former motte and bailey castles at Totternhoe, Cainhoe, and Yelden.

I hope that this book will give pleasure to its readers, and that it will stimulate curiosity in the history and environment of the county.

It is not a comprehensive guide, and unfortunately excludes many interesting places which I have found impossible to cover in this volume.

The drawings can now take up the story, and try to convey the spirit and substance of this intriguing patch of England.

Anthony Mackay
Bedford 1987

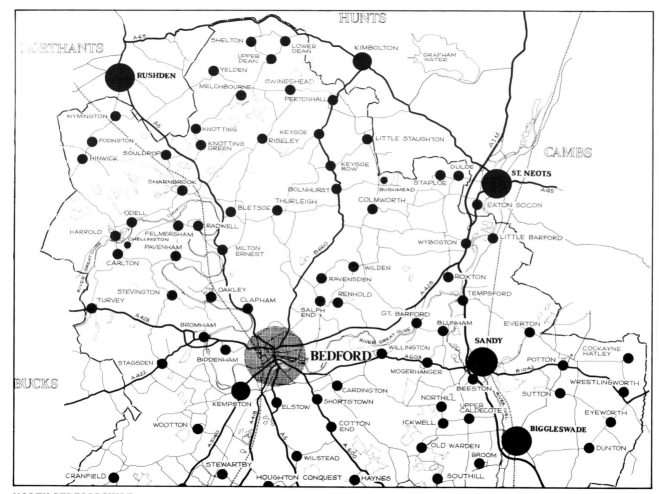

NORTH BEDFORDSHIRE

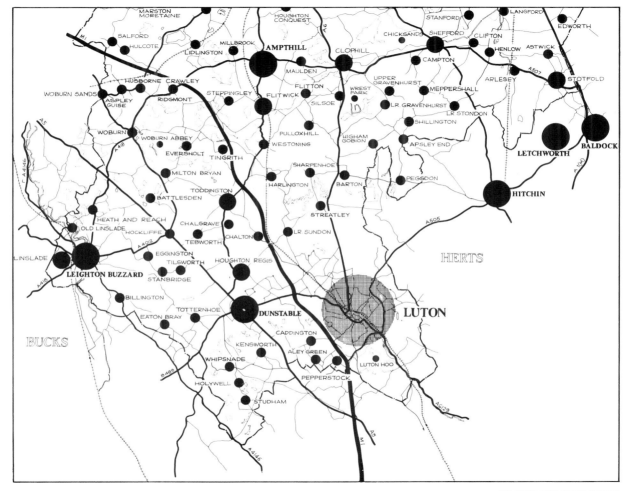

SOUTH BEDFORDSHIRE

TREES NEAR OLD WARDEN

This somewhat bare and lonely tract of countryside is peppered with small, and often beautiful villages, distinguished by elegant church towers and spires, steep-roofed thatched cottages, and several graceful country houses.

Stone buildings west of the Bedford to Rushden road gradually give way to the timber-framed houses of north-east Bedfordshire.

Impressive examples of this construction type can be seen in most villages, but the finest are in Keysoe, and at Basmead Manor in Staploe.

WILDEN CHURCH

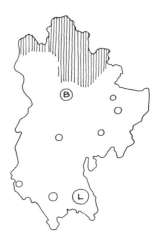

1

PODINGTON : HINWICK : WYMINGTON

Podington is a stone-built village maintained by the Orlebar family of Hinwick, and has a fine church with a leaning 14th-century spire, a Norman chancel and font, a predominantly 13th-century nave, and several monuments to the Orlebars themselves.

Opposite the church are some charming and inventive limestone cottages built in 1773, and many other thatched houses line the village lanes.

Behind Manor Farm lie the remains of a motte and bailey castle which originally had an outer enclosure encircling the whole village.

Hinwick is dignified by the presence of Hinwick House, which was built between 1709 and 1714 for Richard Orlebar, whose family still occupy it. The house stands in magnificent grounds, and has an old lime avenue approach from the east garden. Adjacent to the main house across a courtyard, stands Braye's Manor, a Tudor building converted into stables. The beautiful bell turret built in 1710 is crowned by a cupola.

To the north west of Hinwick House and down the hill is Hinwick Hall, an older building with a west wall dating from 1540, although the east front was built during the 18th century. The avenue leading up to the house from the road is flanked on both sides by water.

Wymington has been largely redeveloped, but has an elegant 13th-century church dominating what remains of the village. It is sited on a raised bank overlooking open country to the west, and has a remarkable east end of decorated embattled treatment with high angled turrets, a two-storeyed south porch, some 14th and 15th-century internal wall paintings, and the earliest brasses in Bedfordshire.

PODINGTON CHURCH

HINWICK HOUSE ▷

2

BRAYE'S MANOR, HINWICK

WYMINGTON CHURCH

YELDEN MOTTE AND BAILEY CASTLE

YELDEN : THE DEANS : SHELTON

Isolated from the main centres of Bedfordshire, these villages lie along the northern county boundary, and are reached from the south by indirect country lanes.

Yelden appears suddenly over a fold in the land, on the approach from Upper Dean, with its Norman motte and bailey castle remains, formerly the stronghold of the Trailly family, in the left-hand field. On the opposite rising bank stands the unusual short broach-spired church of St Mary, in which John Bunyan controversially preached in 1659.

Upper and Lower Dean lie in a gentle leafy valley, separated by about half a mile. Upper Dean has a fine 13th-century church, and an old and ruined tower mill stands on the western outskirts.

Shelton is one of Bedfordshire's most attractive places, an isolated village with an unrestored rustic church, a medieval rectory alongside, and several charming cottages and farms.

SHELTON CHURCH

SWINESHEAD : PERTENHALL : KEYSOE

Swineshead village street is lined with thatched half-timbered or rendered cottages, a magnificent Tudor rectory, and a fine Decorated church with a slender elegant spire.

Pertenhall differs in shape and character, but has an equally charming atmosphere.

Set back behind tall roadside trees, the church stands in a group with the Georgian rectory and the mainly 17th-century Jacobean manor-house.

The village straggles around narrow back lanes, the cottages half-buried behind hedges and bulging flower displays.

As at Swineshead and Pertenhall, *Keysoe* church spire dominates the surrounding landscape, standing on the edge of the village whose cottages are scattered along the Kimbolton road.

Keysoe West has an ancient row of rustic cottages built in wattle and daub, timber-frame and boarding, and brickwork, which seem to have been passed by in the 20th century.

SWINESHEAD VILLAGE STREET

SWINESHEAD RECTORY

KEYSOE CHURCH

DOVECOTE : PERTENHALL

PERTENHALL RECTORY, CHURCH AND MANOR

KEYSOE WEST COTTAGES

BOLNHURST : COLMWORTH
BUSHMEAD : WILDEN

Half a mile away from the village stands the substantial tower of *Bolnhurst* church, a lonely sentinel in the rolling farmland.

Colmworth is strung out along the road, but the church, rectory and Manor Farm cluster in an attractive group, surrounded by trees, and commanding long peaceful views to the east.

North of Colmworth is one of the most interesting buildings in the county. *Bushmead Priory* was founded by Augustinian canons in AD 1195 but the only remains standing are the recently restored refectory buildings, which are now open to the public during summer months.

The attached 18th-century house is all that survives of a much larger house which collapsed during renovations earlier this century.

Wilden village has suffered from too much infill housing recently, but the church of St Nicholas, and the 17th-century manor-house near the gates to the churchyard, make an attractive group.

Several fine half-timbered cottages are dispersed around the village.

BOLNHURST CHURCH

BUSHMEAD PRIORY ▷

12

THURLEIGH : RENHOLD : RAVENSDEN

Clustered on a small hill in undulating country-side, *Thurleigh* church, which shows mainly Perpendicular features, has a Saxon tower crossing, and a Norman carving of Adam and Eve and the tree of knowledge over the south door to the tower.

Bury Hill, just south of the church, is the earth-work of a Norman motte and bailey castle, whose outer enclosure would have encircled the whole village, and whose moat is twenty feet deep and twenty-five feet wide.

A few charming thatched cottages can be seen close to the centre, and to the south west on the Milton Ernest road is a derelict windmill.

Renhold has greatly expanded, but the church, rectory and farm buildings at the eastern end make up a picturesque group nestling amongst the trees. Salph End has been shielded from change, and has the distinctive and very beautiful Abbey Farmhouse, built in the 17th century, and nearby, some rustic looking rendered thatched cottages in good condition.

The lane from Renhold westwards follows a wooded valley on the eastern ridgeline of which stands *Ravensden Church End*. On a delightful site with fine outward views from the well-kept churchyard, the church itself has a magnificent king-post nave roof. Behind the church is a beautiful thatched half-timbered house set back from the road.

The former parish workhouse is now an inn, *The Case is Altered*, which lies in the valley below the church. It has no bar counter within, and the beer is served direct from barrels mounted on a table in the back room. The snug atmosphere of the front rooms is complemented by the tiny garden upon which customers sprawl on warm summer evenings.

THURLEIGH COTTAGES

14

ABBEY FARMHOUSE, SALPH END, RENHOLD

RAVENSDEN CHURCH

16

OAK COTTAGE, CHURCH END, RAVENSDEN ▷

OUSE LANDSCAPE, ROXTON

The river Great Ouse is arguably the county's finest natural asset.

The stretch from the western county boundary at Turvey to the bridge at Bromham flows through a sumptuous landscape, meandering lazily down in sinuous loops over a distance exceeding twenty miles, and embracing a necklace of villages built from the limestone exposed by centuries of flowing water.

In places the river widens into gravel basins, where recent excavations have resulted in glistening lakes, around which wild-life and plant-life reserves have been created.

The river flows at times through woodland, against steep banks, through broad water meadows, under medieval stone arches, and railway bridges built by Victorian engineers to carry the mainline from St Pancras to the north. Its gleaming trail is the dominant feature in this landscape of fields and wild flowers.

Disused watermills stand as testament to the functional role once played by the river, which has now reverted to a simple watercourse.

The villages themselves are distinguished by splendid churches and bridges, and by fine examples of domestic buildings ranging from terraced cottages to refined manor-houses. Although the river no longer supports the activities and crafts practised in the villages, it remains inseparable from them, a constant element in a changing environment.

BIDDENHAM VILLAGE STREET

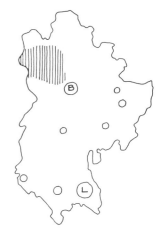

TURVEY

Turvey, with its 13th-century sixteen-arch river bridge acting as a gateway to Bedfordshire from the west, has a winding main street flanked by a rich assortment of stone cottages, almshouses, and public houses, and Turvey Abbey, a beautiful Jacobean house built between 1603 and 1608 on monastic land, and now used as a double monastery by an order of Benedictine monks and nuns.

The Mordaunt family, one of whose members, Lewis, was a judge at the trial of Mary Queen of Scots, lived in Turvey during the 16th and 17th centuries, and is commemorated in the church of All Saints by tomb chests and effigies. The church itself has Saxon nave masonry and tower, with 13th-century additions. The chancel was designed by Sir Giles Gilbert Scott in 1852–54. The south door has exceptional iron scrollwork, similar examples of which can be found at Leighton Buzzard and Eaton Bray, and, in a south aisle recess, can be seen a beautiful early 14th-century painting of the crucifixion. Turvey House, with gardens leading down to the Ouse, was built in 1794, and has an impressive façade.

On a central island of the river, close to the bridge, stand two 18th-century sculptures, one of which is known as Jonah. Nearby, is the first watermill in Bedfordshire, which, although used today by an industrial concern, remains an attractive limestone building.

TURVEY BRIDGE AND PUB

HARROLD BRIDGE

HARROLD

Harrold has two major attractions; the curving medieval stone bridge which twists over the river, with its attached causeway across the water meadows to Carlton, and the Green at the centre of the village, lined with majestic lime trees, surrounded by pretty limestone terraced cottages, and upon which stands an early 18th-century octagonal wooden market cross, and a circular stone lock-up with a conical roof.

The village street has several attractive houses including the Old Manor, dated 1600, and Harrold House, a Victorian Jacobean mansion.

The church of St Peter has a tall perpendicular spire with flying buttresses which signals the presence of Harrold for miles around. This is charmingly complemented by the spire of Chellington church, which stands isolated on rising ground on the opposite bank of the river valley, at about half a mile's distance.

There are fine country walks along the river banks to Odell, through the country park, and past Chellington to Pavenham, with expansive views over the Ouse valley.

CARLTON

Carlton has many delightful 17th-century cottages in the high street and the church of St Mary stands alone on the Turvey road, overlooking the Ouse, and is attended by a group of elegant Scots pine trees. It has several Norman elements in the chancel, but dates principally from the 13th and 14th centuries.

CARLTON CHURCH

ODELL

ODELL CHURCH

This is one of Bedfordshire's most attractive villages, and although there is much new housing woven into its intricate fabric, the villagers have kept up a high standard of planting which softens the effect, and allows old and new to blend comfortably. The *Bell Inn*, at the centre of the village, stands in a row of thatched limestone cottages running down to the old mill on the Ouse, which has now been converted into a house and retains only its waterwheel. On a warm summer evening the inn is a pleasant spot to have a drink, following a walk through the country park.

The church of All Saints, with a lofty and imposing Perpendicular tower, lies on a slope amongst tall sycamores and chestnuts at the edge of the village. On the other side of the road, Odell Castle overlooks the river, on the site of what was once a Norman motte and bailey castle.

HARROLD − ODELL COUNTRY PARK

26

FELMERSHAM

The village is built on raised ground close to the river, the wide flat flood plain extending northwards towards Sharnbrook from the solid early 19th-century bridge. In the plain there is a nature reserve created around a group of pools. This is a protected haven for plantlife, birds and insects, and especially for dragonflies.

In Bedford Museum one can see a collection of Iron Age bronzes and pottery sherds found during gravel excavations just north of the bridge.

The pride of Felmersham is the Early English church standing sentinel close to the river bridge. Distinguished historians have rated this the noblest church in the county, on a par with any abbey or priory church. The west front in particular, with its delicate arcading, deserves special attention, and is best seen as the late evening sunlight streams through the willows on the river banks onto its mellow ageing stonework.

Behind the church is a late medieval tithe barn, and, in the village street, an inn called *The Six Ringers* with a sign showing only five bells.

There is a footpath to Sharnbrook across the river plain.

FELMERSHAM CHURCH

FELMERSHAM BRIDGE

SHARNBROOK : BLETSOE

BLETSOE CHURCH

Sharnbrook has many attractive stone thatched houses in the high street, and an elegant medieval church with a Perpendicular spire with flying buttresses to the corner pinnacles.

Tofte Manor, partly built in 1613, stands on the edge of the village. Sharnbrook mill has been converted to a theatre.

Over the river at high level is a spectacular Victorian railway bridge carrying the mainline from St Pancras to the north.

Bletsoe village is half a mile away from the river, but deserves a mention because of its two principal buildings; the church, and the Elizabethan mansion called Bletsoe Castle. The castle itself is a plain but powerful piece of architecture, and has the remains of a large moat.

The church is beautifully sited amongst twisting chestnut trees, and is best approached along the narrow lane from Thurleigh. It has an interesting monument to Sir John St John dated 1559, kneeling with his wife and nine children. He was related to King Henry VIII, and was brought up under the care of Lady Margaret Beaufort, mother of Henry VII, who was born in the earlier castle building in 1443.

SHARNBROOK VILLAGE GREEN

Radwell has a seven-arch stone bridge built in 1776, and an associated footpath causeway across the flood plain. There is a delightful walk parallel to the river, leading to Pavenham.

Milton Ernest church of All Saints, with its early Norman chancel, 13th-century tower, and Perpendicular clerestory, has an unusual bread cupboard, dated 1729, with three tiers of four-arched pigeon holes each, and a pediment. Restorations in 1864 were by William Butterfield, the celebrated Victorian architect, who also designed the other major building in the village, Milton Ernest Hall, which stands on the river bank.

MILTON ERNEST HALL

PAVENHAM

Pavenham village street is one of the few in Bedfordshire to retain most of the original limestone buildings, and it thereby has a distinctively 17th and 18th-century feel to it. Lying close to the river on rising ground, it once thrived on rush-mat making. The trade has disappeared, but several terraces of plaiters' cottages remain.

The church, which lies on the same hill once occupied by Pavenham Bury, has a fine 13th-century porch, and much Jacobean woodwork.

A beautiful river walk leads out of the village to Stevington.

AVENHAM COTTAGES

RADWELL BRIDGE

33

PAVENHAM RIVER LANDSCAPE

34

STEVINGTON

STEVINGTON WINDMILL

Stevington deserves almost a whole day's visit, there are so many interesting features to study and enjoy. The village boasts a 14th-century stone cross with a finial top, where John Bunyan frequently preached. This is situated at the central crossroads, from where narrow lanes lead away to the ends of the village.

The church of St Mary is sited on a small ridge at the edge of the Ouse plain, and has a Saxon tower crowned by a Perpendicular storey, and inside, early 16th-century poppyheads on the front benches, carved to represent greed, sloth, drinking and learning, and several animal figures. Under the church wall is a Holy Well spring, which was visited by pilgrims in the Middle Ages.

On the south eastern edge of the village is Stevington's magnificently restored windmill, erected in 1770. This postmill was in use until 1930, following rebuilding in 1921, and was totally restored in 1951.

STEVINGTON CHURCH

OAKLEY : CLAPHAM

CLAPHAM CHURCH

The medieval parish church of *Oakley* stands within a few metres of the river amongst tall willows, and has a screen with the only rood loft in the county, and a painting on its coving of Christ on a rainbow. Overlooking the river, Oakley House was remodelled by Henry Holland for the fifth Duke of Bedford, out of a late 17th-century house.

The stone bridge is one of Oakley's finest structures, and makes a picturesque crossing over two humps affording splendid views in both directions along the Ouse valley. A particularly broad and straight stretch of gleaming water flows down from Stevington, whose windmill can be seen on the distant horizon.

There is a fine country walk along the disused railway track towards Stevington and ancient Pictshill.

Clapham is unremarkable except for the church of St Thomas of Canterbury, with its 10th-century Saxon tower, crowned by a Norman top. The original doorway is situated 20 feet up, reminding us that this was once a defensive structure.

OAKLEY BRIDGE

BROMHAM : BIDDENHAM

BROMHAM HALL

Bromham has a 26-arch medieval bridge, partially dating from the 13th-century, and a beautiful 1695 mill which was restored in the 1980s following a disastrous fire. The mill is open to the public, and houses an art gallery on the first floor, and a museum on the ground floor.

Bromham Hall was the home of a prominent Royalist in the Civil War, Sir Lewis Dyve, and is a curious mixture of architectural styles, but sited as it is, low down on the banks of the river, amongst ancient trees and overgrown shrubberies, it exudes an unspoilt atmospheric charm and mellow timelessness.

Within the Park, the church stands alone on high ground, surrounded by its graveyard wall.

The river itself, where it flows under the bridge, attracts herons and kingfishers, and is also a very popular angling spot.

Bromham is the last of the Upper Ouse villages, signalling an end to unnavigable waters, and marking a dramatic change in character as it flows into Kempston and Bedford.

Biddenham is an expanded village, but the older section close to the river, with its stone and thatched cottages and medieval church, retains a delightful rural relationship to the broad pastures which flank the sweeping arc of the Ouse as it approaches Kempston. The village street is wide with grassy verges, and several majestic cedars impart a stately character.

BROMHAM MILL AND BRIDGE

BEDFORD AND THE MARSTON VALE

The Marston Vale stretches from the M1 motorway in the west, to Bedford.

Here the gigantic brick manufacturing industry developed and declined during this century, leaving the brutal scars of extraction across the valley.

In recent years, these pits have become landscape assets, with conversion to sailing and water-skiing lakes.

In the low hills to either side of the Marston Vale, historic villages, medieval churches, and the seats of aristocratic families, reflect the former importance of the area.

It was here that John Bunyan spent much of his life, preaching in the villages, and finding inspiration in the landscape for the settings of 'The Pilgrim's Progress'.

In more recent times, aviation has played an important role in the area, with the Cardington Airship hangars, built for the R100 and R101 in the 1920s, now being used for modern airship construction.

At Cranfield, there is an airfield and the Institute of Technology, and, nearby, the research and development centre of the Royal Aeronautics Establishment in Thurleigh. The Shuttleworth Aircraft Museum and aerodrome at Old Warden is a reminder of the early days of flying.

The river Great Ouse becomes a navigable waterway controlled by new lock-gates to the east of Bedford, where the cluster of villages around its floodplain depend increasingly on market gardening, as the land flattens out.

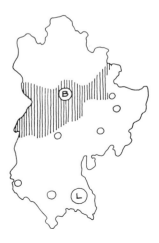

THE RIVER OUSE IN BEDFORD

BEDFORD

Bedford was a market town in Saxon times, and under the Normans, Bedford Castle, of which only the motte remains, was built close to the river bank near the town centre. During the Civil War it was still defended, but thereafter fell into disuse and became a ruin as the town developed.

After occupation by Danish vikings, Edward the Elder reconquered the town, and the King's Ditch, which is still clearly traceable around the southern part of the town centre, was constructed. A series of skirmishes with Danish armies were fought along the Ouse in AD 1009 and AD 1010, before they were eventually repulsed. The only noteworthy medieval remains in Bedford are to be seen in the churches of St Paul on the present market square, St Peter at the north end of the High Street, with its Saxon based tower and Norman south doorway, St Mary to the south of the river bridge, with substantial Saxon and Norman parts in the tower and north transept, and St John nearby, with a Decorated chancel, which was originally the chapel to St John's Hospital next door, remains of which have recently been restored.

In 1794, the Duke of Bedford commissioned Henry Holland to design and build the *Swan Hotel*, into which the 1688 staircase from Houghton House was fitted. Between 1809 and 1812 the bridge across the Ouse was rebuilt by Wing, and the town began to grow appreciably from then onwards.

There are several attractive Regency houses in the town, notably in The Crescent, in Adelaide Square, and in St Mary's Street.

Other buildings of note are the Dame Alice Street almshouses, the High School, several buildings in Mill Street including the Bunyan Meeting House, John Howard's House, the former fire station, and a fine Georgian house next door. In the market square, the Shire Hall, the old part of the Town Hall, and the upper part of the former Lloyds Bank building, are elegant buildings.

Bedford's most beautiful feature is the Embankment, with its magnificent tree-lined walks and gardens. From the town centre one can follow routes in both directions along the river banks, and reach open country within a short time, passing through glades of willows, over footbridges, around lakes created out of former gravel workings, and eventually into open fields.

Bedford is a notable rowing centre, and holds a spectacular regatta on the Ouse every summer.

◁ *BEDFORD BRIDGE*   *THE MARKET PLACE*

ST PETERS CHURCH FONT

SWAN HOTEL

THE EMBANKMENT ▷

FROM NEWNHAM FOOTBRIDGE

KEMPSTON

Kempston has merged physically with Bedford, but has a few distinctive corners, such as the Norman church with Perpendicular tower and nave at Church End, the *King William IV* timber-framed pub, and several thatched cottages tucked away behind it. There are footpaths leading to Bedford and Biddenham, and the river is ideal for canoeing.

KING WILLIAM IV PUB

MARSTON MORETAINE : SALFORD : CRANFIELD : WOOTTON : HULCOTE : STAGSDEN : MILLBROOK

Marston Moretaine church of St Mary has a detached tower, a finely vaulted vestry and chancel, and pews with tracery and linenfolds.

Moat Farm with an Elizabethan west end, has recently been renovated and turned into a restaurant. The interior ceilings have particularly attractive exposed timber structures.

Salford, Cranfield and Wootton have been expanded in recent years, and retain only a few traditional cottages.

Hulcote, however, within a stone's throw of the M1, is a surprisingly peaceful and beautiful hamlet, with a tiny Elizabethan church on a small hill approached along an avenue of lime trees. Rebuilt in 1590, it is the smallest of its period in England, and contains a family monument to the Chernockes (1615). Opposite the church is a fine yellow brick former rectory of late Georgian times.

Stagsden village is overpowered by heavy traffic navigating its tight bends, and yet possesses several attractive thatched cottages, a smithy, and a Decorated church with Perpendicular additions, set back amongst tall trees. There is also a Bird Garden at the foot of the winding lane leading to Stevington.

Millbrook is located in a beautiful wooded combe of the Greensand Ridge, and the picturesque church stands prominently on a hill, overlooking the Marston Vale. Bunyan's 'Valley of the Shadow' is reputedly based on this combe.

MARSTON MORETAINE MOATED MANOR

MILLBROOK BRICKWORKS

HULCOTE CHURCH

ELSTOW MOOT HALL

HOUGHTON CONQUEST :
ELSTOW

Houghton Conquest was named after the Conquest family, who lived in the manor house from the 13th to 18th centuries.

The church of All Saints has many distinguishing features including a beautiful Perpendicular south doorway, a large 14th-century painting of Christ over the chancel arch, and pieces of original stained glass throughout.

The mid-18th-century rectory is approached up a splendid lime avenue, and is now a private house.

Elstow is interesting, not only because of associations with John Bunyan, the Puritan preacher and writer, but because it possesses some exquisite buildings grouped around one of the most relaxed and serene of Bedfordshire's village greens.

The present church is all that remains of a former Benedictine nunnery, which was founded about 1075 by a niece of William the Conqueror, became one of the wealthiest in the country, was surrendered to King Henry VIII in 1539, and in 1616, passed into the hands of Thomas Hillersdon, who built Elstow Place on adjacent ground out of stone taken from domestic parts of the Abbey. The ruins of this house, and its approach driveway from the east, can be seen today.

The church itself has a detached campanile similar to that in Marston Moretaine, and has Norman arches, a 13th-century rib-vaulted chapter house, and several fine brasses and monuments. The traceried Perpendicular pulpit has been removed to the Moot Hall museum.

The timber-framed Moot Hall standing on the green, was built in about 1500, and had shops on the ground floor, with a court or meeting room above. It is now a Bunyan museum.

Many cottages in the village have recently been renovated exposing substantial timber frames.

51

◁ *FORMER RECTORY, HOUGHTON CONQUEST*

ELSTOW GREEN

ELSTOW ABBEY CHURCH AND HILLERSDON MANOR

CARDINGTON HANGARS

CARDINGTON :
WILLINGTON : COTTON END

At *Cardington*, the gigantic hangars built to construct the famous airships of the 1920s, dominate the skyline, and the village itself remains a charming place, with church, major houses and simple cottages grouped around the green.

In the 18th century the Whitbread family and John Howard, the prison reformer, lived here.

Willington lies close to the Ouse, where remains of Viking earthworks can be seen. It was here that the Danes moored their ships, whilst mounting attacks on Bedford in the 10th and early 11th centuries.

The Dovecote and Stable buildings, erected about 1536, are open to the public. These are all that remain of Sir John Gostwick's manor-house, in which he entertained Henry VIII in 1541. The church is late Perpendicular, and built of beautiful golden stone. There are extensive walks through the poplar woods bordering the river, which are spectacular in spring and autumn.

In *Cotton End* are two outstanding houses; Herrings Green Farm and Manor Farm, a solid and imposing tudor building.

55

◁ *HOWARD'S HOUSE, CARDINGTON*

WILLINGTON DOVECOTE AND STABLES

MANOR FARM, COTTON END

GREAT BARFORD :
ROXTON : TEMPSFORD :
BLUNHAM : MOGERHANGER

The pride of *Great Barford* is the 17-arch, 15th-century bridge over the Ouse, which is complemented at one end by the picturesque grouping of pinnacled church, and white-painted inn. The river itself is particularly beautiful on its western approaches to the bridge, as it flows through tree-lined meadows and reed beds.

Roxton is a small village with several thatched cottages, and an unusual Nonconformist chapel.

Each year in the grounds of Roxton House, a large traction engine rally takes place, attracting thousands of visitors.

Lying within a few metres of the A1, the hamlet of *Tempsford Church End* has a fine 15th-century timber-framed house next to the church, a beautiful 18th-century farm with magnificent barns, and the overgrown remains of Gannock's castle, a medieval fortified farmstead. The AD 917 attack on Bedford was launched from near Tempsford.

Blunham has several old buildings grouped around the church including a 16th-century manor-house, thatched cottages, and a Baptist chapel built in 1751.

The metaphysical poet, Dr John Donne was rector of the church from 1621 to 1631. From here it is possible to ramble along the disused Oxford to Cambridge railway track to Bedford.

At *Mogerhanger* Sir John Soane designed Mogerhanger Park in 1791–1809, and a fine view of this elegant white-painted house can be had from the lane leading south out of the village.

ROXTON CONGREGATIONAL CHAPEL

GREAT BARFORD BRIDGE

GANNOCKS, TEMPSFORD

BLUNHAM VILLAGE

62

THE EAST

The Great North Road defines the western edge of the region.

The undulating countryside of central Bedfordshire tails off in a final flourish of the Greensand ridge at Sandy, and gives way to large fields and flat expanses in the approaches to Cambridge-shire.

This is a land of broad, wind-blown skies, of farms huddled for shelter against stands of trees, of meadows of yellow rape and scarlet poppies, and of distinctive Church towers ranging from the stumpy flintstone mass of Wrestlingworth to the soaring pinnacles of Cockayne Hatley.

BIGGLESWADE

SANDY : EVERTON : POTTON
SUTTON : COCKAYNE HATLEY

Sandy is a centre for market gardening, and some of the most remarkable buildings in the area are the massed ranks of greenhouses dispersed across the flat fertile Ivel valley. The heavily wooded ridge which forms a backcloth to the town, has remains of Iron Age earthworks, and the headquarters of the RSPB which provides a nature reserve with trails open to the public. The Lodge, once the home of Sir Robert Peel's son, William, has beautiful gardens with formal pools.

Hasell's Hall, built between 1720 and 1740 with additions in 1780, is set in elegant parkland.

Everton village has some rustic looking thatched cottages perched on the slope of a low ridge, with long views opening up to the north.

Potton market-place contains several brick Georgian houses and hotels, and the Decorated church is situated on a small hill on the eastern fringe of the village.

Not far from Potton the small hamlet of *Sutton* has one of the most delightful groups of buildings in Bedfordshire, centred around the church and rectory, and overlooking a stream spanned by a rare 15th-century packhorse bridge with a ford alongside.

The tall isolated tower of *Cockayne Hatley* is a finely detailed Perpendicular landmark in the increasingly flat landscape on the county boundary.

SUTTON PACKHORSE BRIDGE

SANDY WOODS ▷

64

COCKAYNE HATLEY CHURCH

66

WRESTLINGWORTH : EYEWORTH : EDWORTH : BIGGLESWADE

Wrestlingworth has a snug little inn and several typical thatched cottages around the stubby brown cobbled church tower, and *Eyeworth* and *Edworth* both have charming little churches in extremely rural settings.

The Beaumont farmhouse in Edworth was the home of Agnes Beaumont, who was the subject of a minor scandal in 1647 involving John Bunyan, in which he was accused of assisting to poison her father, and for which he was absolved at an inquest.

Biggleswade lies alongside the Great North Road, and was a flourishing coaching town in the 18th-century. The former Town Hall built in 1844, is one of its finest buildings, but much of the town was rebuilt after the disastrous fire of 1785, and only small traces of the Tudor and Georgian fabric show through today.

WRESTLINGWORTH CHURCH

EYEWORTH CHURCH

This is a beautiful stretch of countryside, a perfect blend of the wild and the picturesque.

The villages of Southill, Ickwell, Northill, and Old Warden nestle in the densely wooded folds of the Greensand as it peters out against the broad acres of the River Ivel.

From various vantage points in the hills, long views open up towards the east, across the market gardening region of the county.

Amongst the highlights of the area are the Shuttleworth Aircraft Museum with its summer displays of early aeroplanes; the delightful thatched cottages and model village buildings of Old Warden; the Maypole dancing and village cricket matches on Ickwell Green; the majestic splendour of Southill Park, and the charming nucleus of church, pub and duckpond at Northill.

The woods and fields are made accessible by a fine network of footpaths and trails.

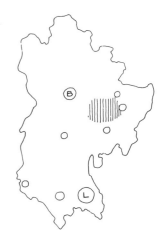

NORTHILL COTTAGE AND CHURCH

OLD WARDEN

Old Warden itself is a model village, built for Lord Ongley during the 19th-century around a main street lined with thatched, or decoratively tiled cottages, a pub, a shop, and a school, sited to one side on a rising bank crowned by dense woodland, and to the other, in a cosy hollow merging into lush meadows and small coppices.

Each house is slightly different in decoration and detail, but the buff coloured paint-wash used, and the consistent white-painted woodwork, maintain a family resemblance, and unify the intricately planned village.

In and around Warden Warren are thatched lodges and estate workers' cottages, punctuating several splendid walking trails.

At the northern end of the village on Quint's Hill, stands the 12th-century, much-restored church, whose churchyard commands long views over Warden Park to the east, and from where there are good walks leading to Warden Abbey. Founded in AD 1135, the only remains are part of the Gostwicks' 1537 house, with twisted Tudor chimney stacks and decorative brickwork, and several dried-out fishponds used by the original Cistercian monks.

The Shuttleworth Museum hosts nostalgic flying displays throughout the summer months, and houses a collection of early aircraft.

OLD WARDEN THATCHED COTTAGE

OLD WARDEN VILLAGE STREET ▷

WARDEN ABBEY REMAINS

NORTHILL POND, PUB AND CHURCH

ICKWELL : NORTHILL : SOUTHILL : COPLE

The nearby hamlet of *Ickwell* is a collection of pretty cottages nestling around a spacious green, with a maypole, and a cricket pitch with an old oak tree close to the wicket. On a warm summer's evening with a game in progress, the atmosphere is memorable. On May Day, dancing and a country fair are staged on the green.

Northill, half a mile away, has a beautiful group of church, pub and thatched cottages, around a small duckpond, and an elegant Queen Anne house Northill Grange, stands facing the approach from Cople.

Southill village revolves around the majestic Southill Park, standing in grounds landscaped by Capability Brown in 1777. The house was built for the Byng family in the mid-18th-century, and remodelled by Holland between 1796 and 1801 for Samuel Whitbread, the brewer and MP for Bedford, whose family have lived there ever since. It must rank as one of England's most beautiful houses.

As at Old Warden, there are many thatched estate cottages in the village, built at the close of the 18th century, and a late medieval church is set back from the road against the woods of Southill Park, and amongst mellowed high-walled nursery gardens.

From the hamlet of Ireland, one can walk along the disused Hitchin to Bedford railway track, through cuttings bursting with wild flowers.

Cople

The church is notable for its distinctive 15th and 16th-century brasses and the traceried screen. A gabled 17th-century house opposite the church is well maintained.

73

ICKWELL COTTAGES

SOUTH FRONT, SOUTHILL PARK ▷

SOUTHILL CHURCH

WOBURN ABBEY AND SURROUNDING VILLAGES

Woburn Abbey is one of England's finest stately homes, enfolded by wooded hills, and overlooking broad, sweeping deerpark, falling towards the town of Woburn, whose church towers can be seen over trees surrounding the lakes and gardens bordering the western edge of the park.

In AD 1145, a Cistercian abbey was founded at Woburn by Hugh de Bolebec of Fountains, and was granted in 1547 to John Lord Russell, who became the first Earl of Bedford, and whose descendants still live there.

Nothing remains of the original abbey, and the present buildings date from the late 17th and 18th centuries, erected to designs by Flitcroft and Holland.

Today the Abbey is open to the public and linked to the Wildlife Animal Kingdom.

Other interesting features include the Chinese Dairy, a Chinese Temple in a maze, and an antiques centre.

Several villages in the vicinity of the Abbey, including Husborne Crawley, Lidlington, Ridgmont, and Woburn town itself, have numerous cottages built to house workers on the estate, where the Duke of Bedford had about 450 employees in the mid-19th-century.

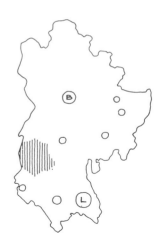

WOBURN

◁ *WEST FRONT, WOBURN ABBEY*

WOBURN ABBEY AND PARK

EAST FRONT, WOBURN ABBEY

WOBURN

The town of *Woburn* was largely rebuilt in the 18th century following damaging fires in 1595 and 1724, and the effects of Civil War plundering. The main street is lined on both sides by a succession of elegant Georgian houses and shopfronts, and has several attractive inns. At the crossroads an unusual neo-gothic market house designed by Blore, the architect of the façade to the former Bedford Modern School, stands on its own, with the main footpath running through the alleyway created behind it. Pavements are decoratively constructed of brown cobbles and flat stone slabs, and are enriched by painted ironwork railings, and colourful planting in tubs and window-boxes.

Woburn is architecturally the most distinguished town in Bedfordshire, and is exceptionally well maintained.

WOBURN MARKET HOUSE

RIDGMONT : ASPLEY GUISE : HUSBORNE CRAWLEY

Ridgmont stands on the edge of the Greensand Ridge, and commands extensive views towards Aspley Guise and the new city of Milton Keynes. It is typical of the Bedford estate villages, with its gabled brick houses.

A footpath across the fields leads to ruined Segenhoe church, with its early Norman chancel and south doorway, and there is a clear view from here of the tall spire of the Scott-designed church of All Saints back in the village.

The adjacent villages of *Aspley Guise* and *Husborne Crawley* both contain buildings of note, and Aspley Heath, which rises on the wooded sandy ridge behind, is a beautiful place for walking at any time of the year.

Aspley House, dated 1695, is attributed to Wren, and stands in splendid gardens. Guise House is early 18th-century, and Old House is Elizabethan, dating from 1575.

In the centre of the village, the former market place has a picturesque shelter and tightly arranged houses and shops clustered around it.

Close to the church on the hill in Husborne Crawley, is an Elizabethan farmhouse, and several cottages of individual, if somewhat eccentric, character. In the grounds of 18th-century Crawley Park, are some half-timbered thatched estate houses.

◁ *WOBURN HIGH STREET*

CRAWLEY PARK COTTAGES

EVERSHOLT : MILTON
BRYAN : BATTLESDEN

Eversholt, with several Ends, lies immediately east of Woburn Park, and boasts some exceptionally fine timber-framed houses. The church is mainly Perpendicular, but has Norman and Early English work in the north arcade.

At *Milton Bryan* the designer of the Crystal Palace, Sir Joseph Paxton, was born, and he is commemorated by a window in the church. As a young man he worked at *Battlesden Park*. Battlesden is an isolated hamlet now, with only a disused, but hauntingly nostalgic church, sited in a small hollow in the hill, and overlooking low-lying meadows stretching towards the chalk uplands of Totternhoe and Dunstable.

BATTLESDEN CHURCH

84

TYRELL'S END COTTAGE, EVERSHOLT

WITTS END CLOSE, EVERSHOLT

MILTON BRYAN FORMER POST OFFICE ▷

WOBURN TREES

THE GREENSAND, FLIT AND GAULT

The central reaches of the Greensand hills encompassing Ampthill, Maulden, Haynes and Clophill, are steeply sloping on their northern face, creating surprisingly dramatic, elevated views over the Marston Vale and Bedford.

The western end of this gentle ridge tumbles down from poetic sounding Breakheart, Moneypot, and Jackdaw Hills, through dense woodland to the flat valley below. Ampthill nestles in the hills. Beyond Maulden, dense forest appears again, before the Greensand dies away to the east of Clophill.

The south side of the Greensand is defined by the fertile River Flit valley, running eastwards to join the Ivel near Biggleswade.

South of the river, the ground rises gently onto the Gault clay, and into one of the most charming rural areas of Bedfordshire, with a cluster of villages including Flitton, Silsoe, Shillington, the Gravenhursts and Campton, and with magnificent Wrest Park as its focal point, and the steeply rising Barton Hills providing a dramatic backcloth to the south.

Further to the east the land flattens into the Ivel valley, and is somewhat dull country, although there are isolated buildings and buried corners worth visiting, such as Astwick, with its unique church tower and moated Bury Farm; the water meadows near Langford, and the park at Henlow Grange.

HOUGHTON HOUSE, AMPTHILL

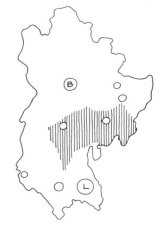

AMPTHILL

Ampthill has retained a distinctly 18th-century character, and the streets fanning out from the central crossroads are lined with superb examples, including Avenue House, Dynevor House, and Brandreth House in Church Street, and the *White Hart Inn* and several houses in Dunstable Street.

The 19th-century Moot Hall with picturesque cupola and fanciful gables, the Obelisk Pump engraved as a signpost, and an old market building nearby make an engaging group on the crossroads itself.

On Woburn Street a small estate of thatched cottages built between 1812 and 1816, timber-framed and infilled with brick, stand against the wooded backdrop of the park. The park is on high ground, and was the site of Ampthill Castle, where Katherine of Aragon stayed, and who is commemorated by a stone cross. There are footpaths through the woods with occasional panoramic views from the steep north side.

Ampthill Park House, a beautiful late 17th-century building, was extended and decorated by Chambers in about 1790, and has fine avenues of trees on the north side.

Houghton House is sited dramatically to overlook the Marston Valley, and has a chequered history which has left it in ruins. Built in 1615 for Lady Pembroke, it passed through several hands before the Duke of Bedford bought it in 1738, and a later Duke dismantled it in 1794. The Tuscan-columned west front loggia is attributed to Inigo Jones. The staircase was removed to the *Swan Hotel* in Bedford. It is classed as an Ancient Monument and is open to the public, and is certainly one of the most intriguing and beautiful places in the county.

AMPTHILL PARK

WEST FACADE, HOUGHTON HOUSE

AMPTHILL COTTAGES

AMPTHILL CHURCH/LANDSCAPE

MAULDEN : CLOPHILL :
CHICKSANDS : HAYNES

Maulden, has a few picturesque cottages around the village green, but is attractive mainly for the forest walks in neighbouring Maulden Wood.

Clophill's main street is lined with a variety of interesting houses, and has a ruined medieval church standing alone on rising ground to the north of the village, with views towards the space age antenna on the American base at Chicksands. The contrast of old and new here is particularly poignant.

Across the River Flit are the remains of the Castle of Cainhoe, a Norman motte and bailey structure built for the D'Albini family, which came to England with William the Conqueror, and was one of the major baronies in Bedfordshire.

Chicksands Priory was founded in AD 1150 for monks and nuns of the Gilbertine monastic order. The remains are limited to an Early English doorway, a 15th-century oriel window, a vaulted undercroft, and part of the perpendicular cloisters. The house was remodelled by James Wyatt in 1813, and is now part of the RAF/USAF base, and is sometimes open to the public.

Haynes is a village of ends, in which there are assorted timbered cottages, a heavily restored church, and an 18th-century mansion now functioning as a girls' boarding school.

CHICKSANDS PRIORY

96

CLOPHILL COTTAGES

FLITWICK : FLITTON

Flitwick is undistinguished save for the mill, and the manor close to the church, but the villages of *Flitton* and *Silsoe* both have many interesting houses, and the church of St John Baptist in Flitton has a mausoleum to the Grey family of Wrest Park.

FLITTON COTTAGES

◁ *CAINHOE CASTLE MOUND*

SILSOE

Wrest Park House itself was built between 1834 and 1836 to designs by the Earl de Grey. It stands in formal gardens which are open to the public during the summer months, and in which are an Orangery, a Bath House, a bowling green and pavilion, and at the end of a long central pool, a domed pavilion designed in 1711 by Thomas Archer. The gardens have many fine trees, and statues punctuate the woodland pathways.

SILSOE COTTAGES

SOUTH FRONT, WREST PARK ▷

CAMPTON : MEPPERSHALL : SHILLINGTON : GRAVENHURST

Campton, close to Shefford, has an Elizabethan manor-house built in 1591, with a magnificent front of five gables and a central porch. It stands back from the road at the end of a driveway lined with mature trees.

On the opposite side of the road is a simple 18th-century former rectory.

Meppershall church, and the early 17th-century manor-house nearby, with the remains of a Norman motte and bailey castle in its grounds, stand on high ground, with views over rolling farmland to the towers of adjacent village churches. At a junction in the village is one of the finest thatched timber-framed cottages in the county, and on the eastern outskirts is St Thomas a' Becket's Chapel, dated between 1170 and 1180, with a late Norman doorway, and which belonged to Chicksands Priory.

Shillington church tower dominates the valleys around, both by its size and the prominence of the hilltop site around which the village clusters. At Upton, Bury, and Apsley Ends, are many examples of mid-Bedfordshire half-timbered thatched cottages.

However, Pirton Grange, hidden behind a stand of dense trees, with its moat and gatehouse intact, and showing evidence of construction from Elizabethan, Jacobean and Georgian times, is one of the jewels of the county, even though, strictly speaking, the house lies in neighbouring Hertfordshire, and part of the moat in Bedfordshire.

Situated in undulating countryside, *Gravenhurst* is divided into Upper and Lower villages, and boasts two fine ironstone churches, and several old cottages and farmhouses.

SHILLINGTON VILLAGE STREET

CAMPTON MANOR

MEPPERSHALL MANOR

104

MEPPERSHALL THATCHED COTTAGE

LITTLE ION FARM, GRAVENHURST

SHILLINGTON CHURCH ▷

APSLEY END THATCHED COTTAGE

PIRTON GRANGE ▷

HENLOW : STOTFOLD : ASTWICK

Henlow has several fine 17th-century houses along the High Street, and the largely perpendicular church stands across a sunken green.

Henlow Grange, lying in parkland close to the River Hiz, was built about AD 1770, and is now a beauty/health centre.

In *Stotfold*, Ivy Cottage is one of the few outstanding buildings remaining.

Astwick, an isolated and peaceful hamlet, apparently unaffected by its proximity to the A1, has the beautiful Church Farm, and moated Bury Farm.

The church of St Guthlac has a mysterious stunted tower with traces of unresolved arch construction on its south face. Rectory House, dated 1720, stands to the north of the church.

HENLOW CHURCH

BURY FARM : ASTWICK

111

IVY COTTAGE, STOTFOLD

THE WEST

The west includes the flat valley stretching from Watling Street to Leighton Linslade, bounded by the chalk hills of the Chilterns to the south, and the sandy or clay hills to the north and east.

In an undistinguished landscape, several individual buildings and villages stand out; the half-timbered houses of Harlington; the varied buildings grouped around the Green at Toddington; the stubby church at Chalgrave, solitary in a small stand of trees; the village of Totternhoe, strung out beneath the Knolls, a former motte and bailey castle; the powerful 15th-century stone gatehouse to moated Tilsworth Manor; the beautiful Queen Anne house at Eggington; and the nostalgic site of the castle at Eaton Bray, built in AD 1221. These are just some of the gems of the west.

Dominating the valley is the church of Leighton Buzzard. Beyond the town stretches the rolling plain of Buckinghamshire.

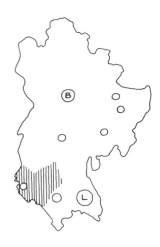

TODDINGTON CHURCH AND COTTAGES

LEIGHTON BUZZARD :
LINSLADE :
HEATH AND REACH

Leighton Buzzard is a large and flourishing market town on either side of the River Ouzel and the Grand Junction Canal, and has a wide High Street with the market stalls set out along both sides, and up to the 15th-century pinnacled cross. There are many fine 17th, 18th and 19th-century houses and hotels both here, and in Church Square.

The church of All Saints is a large cruciform building with an impressive high Early English spire, visible for miles around. The chancel has a beautiful screen and stalls with complete misericords with heads and foliage. The west door displays 13th-century ironwork, probably made by Thomas of Leighton, who also made the grille for Queen Eleanor's tomb in Westminster Abbey in 1294.

At *Old Linslade* there is a charming group of church, manor-house, canal and river bridges, and nearby, in a green and pleasant valley alongside the canal is the *Globe Inn.*

Heath and Reach lies amongst woods and sandy hills, and has some attractive half-timbered, thatched cottages grouped with the pub, clock-tower, and lock-up, around a small green.

LEIGHTON BUZZARD MARKET CROSS

THE GLOBE, OLD LINSLADE ▷

114

HEATH AND REACH COTTAGES

EAST FROM HOCKLIFFE CHURCH

Eggington, Tilsworth and *Stanbridge* all have interesting parish churches, but the outstanding buildings of interest in this group are late 17th-century Eggington House, the 15th-century ironstone gatehouse to Tilsworth Manor Farm, and the converted tower mill at Stanbridge.

The small church of St Nicholas at *Hockliffe*, overlooks an exquisite stretch of countryside between it and Leighton Buzzard, and there are footpath connections across the fields past Hockliffe Grange.

TILSWORTH MANOR

EATON BRAY : TOTTERNHOE

Eaton Bray had a castle built in 1221 in the flat meadows about half a mile to the west of the village, where remains of the moat can be seen. The church of St Mary has two of the finest Early English arcades in the country, dated about 1220 and 1240, and marvellous wrought iron scrolls on the south door dating from the mid-13th-century.

Totternhoe village lines up along the foot of the Knolls with the Perpendicular church, built of the local stone, situated at the southern end. Atop the Knolls are the remains of a substantial Norman motte and bailey castle, originally a Bronze Age site, and now a nature reserve for chalk flora. The manor-house of Lancotbury is a beautiful timber-framed 16th-century building.

TOTTERNHOE KNOLLS

119

WHITBREAD

CROSS KEYS, TOTTERNHOE

CHALGRAVE CHURCH

TODDINGTON :
HARLINGTON : SUNDON :
CHALGRAVE

Toddington is built around a large sloping green, and has many elegant houses, in particular, Wentworth House, dated 1700, of chequered brickwork. The church crowns the hill, and is impressive with its battlements and decorated cornice depicting various animals and birds.

To the north of the village lies Toddington Manor, built between 1570 and 1580. Only the kitchen block remains of the original house, as all the rest was erected after 1745. It was the home of Henrietta, Baroness Wentworth in 1667, and was the scene of an ill-fated love affair with the Duke of Monmouth, who made an abortive attempt on the throne in 1685, ending in his execution, and the subsequent heartbroken death of the Baroness.

The village of *Harlington* stands on top of a hill overlooking the plain towards Leighton Buzzard in the west, and the delightful hills of Sundon and Sharpenhoe to the east.

The manor housed the magistrates court which tried John Bunyan in 1660, and has fine Tudor interiors. There are several prominent timber-framed houses in the village, clustered near the church.

Sundon has an extremely fine decorated church standing amongst large chestnuts and limes at the lower end of the village.

Chalgrave is thought to have been a large village at one time, but the only remains now are the church and a farm nearby.

The church tower fell down during a storm in 1889, and has never been rebuilt. Surrounded by a fine group of horse-chestnut trees, the church stands isolated on the outskirts of Toddington, with fine views from here to the Chilterns.

HARLINGTON PUB

SUNDON HILLS FROM HARLINGTON ▷

LOWER SUNDON CHURCH

124

Luton and Dunstable lie in a break in the Chilterns, and have merged into one continuous urban whole during the 20th century.

The Chilterns splutter across the southern boundary of Bedfordshire, creating a variety of upland scenery. The bare Downs above Dunstable give way to heavily wooded contours around Whipsnade, Studham, and Kensworth, and rise again east of Luton as Warden Hill, with the Iron Age and Bronze Age remains at Dray's Ditches, and the barrows of Galley Hill beyond. The beautiful Barton Hills terminate the chalk downs in Deacon Hill at Pegsdon. These hills are partly composed of rounded bare humps, but in the valleys cutting into the steep northern face above Barton-le-Clay, dense woods line the slopes and lower ridges.

At Sharpenhoe Clappers, which is National Trust land, a spectacular beech wood crowns the prominent hilltop, and beyond, towards Sundon, is some of the most delightful countryside in Bedfordshire, where the fields of the Gault reach into the rippling indentations of the hills, creating combes and spurs in the process.

It is said that these hills are the 'Delectable Mountains' of Bunyan's 'The Pilgrim's Progress', and it is difficult to dispute the possibility.

HOUGHTON REGIS CHURCH

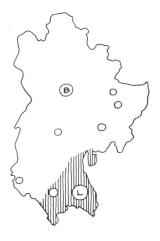

LUTON : HOUGHTON REGIS

Luton grew during the 19th century through the straw hat industry, and more recently the motor industry, but although attractively sited in a break in the chalk hills, is not a beautiful town. Its main attractions are the church of St Mary, Someries Castle, and Luton Hoo.

St Mary's is a large and very fine parish church with Norman and Early English capitals and arches, but was mostly built in the 13th and 14th centuries with later Perpendicular additions. Its octagonal baptistry, dated 1340, and double-arched screen of 1461, are exceptional features. The church squats uncomfortably amongst tall trees on a cramped site, surrounded by threatening and ugly buildings on three sides, but it still proudly outshines them.

At Someries, are the remains of a 15th-century brick gatehouse, situated on a deserted hill about two miles to the south-west of the town.

Luton Hoo was designed by Robert Adam in 1763, finished by Smirke in 1827, and a fire gutted the building in 1843. The remodelling was carried out by Mewes, of the French architects who designed the Ritz in London. The house contains a fascinating collection from the family of the Csars of Russia. The park extends over downland, and was landscaped by Capability Brown. Its main features are two long lakes and many magnificent trees. The rose garden on the south front is enclosed by a sweeping yew hedge with domed stone pavilions at the corners.

Houghton Regis lies between Luton and Dunstable. Houghton Hall, a Queen Anne brick mansion dated 1700, stands in parkland at the town centre, a distinguished but lonely remnant of a more elegant past. The 20th-century has witnessed massive housing expansion, leaving only a few old houses close to the stately medieval church of All Saints.

ST MARY'S CHURCH, LUTON

SOMERIES CASTLE GATEHOUSE

◁ *SOUTH GARDENS, LUTON HOO*

SOUTH FRONT, LUTON HOO

SHARPENHOE : BARTON

Sharpenhoe Clappers is a particularly attractive spur covered by a graceful stand of beeches. Views from here towards Barton and to the north are amongst the most beautiful in the county.

Barton-le-Clay is tucked against the foot of steeply rising hills, and has several 17th and 18th-century houses grouped along the approach lane to the church. From here, footpaths up onto the Barton Hills pass through a wooded valley before emerging into grassy uplands, where once again the views are spectacular. On the west side of the village lies an old moated farm called Faldo.

From Dray's Ditches beneath Warden Hill, there is a walk along the ancient Icknield Way, over Galley Hill and Telegraph Hill to Deacon Hill. This is a romantic and historic pathway, once one of the principal routes of pre-Roman Britain, and now overgrown, lined with majestic beech trees, and preserved as a bridleway and footpath.

SHARPENHOE CLAPPERS WOODS

THE BARTON HILLS

SUNDON HILLS

NEAR TELEGRAPH HILL, THE ICKNIELD WAY

SHARPENHOE CLAPPERS

MARSHE ALMSHOUSES

DUNSTABLE

The earliest indications of settlement near *Dunstable* are the Neolithic and Bronze Age barrows on the Downs, but it started to grow on the present site around the crossing of Roman Watling Street and the Icknield Way.

It was an important monastic centre during the Middle Ages, and thereafter became one of the principal coaching towns on the main road out of London, before the straw hat industry in the 19th century, and the motor industry in this century, transformed it from a small market town, to a sizeable commercial centre.

The Priory Church of St Peter is undoubtedly the finest ecclesiastical building in Bedfordshire, consisting of a seven-bay Norman nave with massive fluted and incised columns, and a complex, but intriguing, west front composed of Norman and Early English elements. The church is built from very attractive golden limestone, and has chequered patternwork in the 15th-century north west tower.

The Priory was founded in 1132 by King Henry I, and was an important religious centre during the 13th and 14th centuries. It was used by the court which pronounced divorce judgement against Katherine of Aragon, the first wife of Henry VIII, and was visited by many kings and queens during the next few centuries.

It stands close to the town centre on a raised mound surrounded by fine trees, and opposite the Old Palace Hotel, which is on the site of 12th-century Kingsbury Manor, and the elegant Marshe Almshouses built in 1745.

Close to where Watling Street cuts through the chalk ridge at the northern approach to Dunstable, are the remains of an Iron Age hillfort at Maiden Bower.

This is partly damaged by quarrying, but is nevertheless on a dramatic elevated site overlooking the gentle green valley to the north. To the west are the uneven humps of Totternhoe Knolls with its Norman castle remains. There are interesting nature walks along the disused railway cutting below.

The Downs offer many fine walks and horse rides, with splendid views to the hills of Buckinghamshire, and have become the venue for gliding and hang-gliding off the steep northwest face.

WHIPSNADE : STUDHAM
KENSWORTH : CADDINGTON

Whipsnade is famous for the zoo established on the Downs in 1931, and is also a pretty village scattered around a spacious common, with a 'Tree Cathedral' whose rights belong to the National Trust. Within the zoo, which is perched around the rim of the chalk ridge, are several Lubetkin-designed white concrete buildings, erected during the 1930s, and which represent the only examples of modern architecture in the whole county.

Studham is also dispersed around a common and its church has fine arcades dated between 1210 and 1220.

Kensworth has some beautiful half-timbered houses at Kensworth Lynch, and the church stands amongst mature trees in a charming rural setting.

All three villages are linked by footpaths connecting their commons, and making an interesting day's walking.

Caddington, high on the Downs, has an attractive church, the tower of which is built of stone, flint and brick. Several hamlets on the county boundary have unusual names like Aley Green, Pepperstock and Slip End.

KENSWORTH CHURCH

138

WHIPSNADE CHURCH AND FARM

STUDHAM VILLAGE STREET

BIBLIOGRAPHY

Bedfordshire, Huntingdon and Peterborough : Nikolaus Pevsner : Penguin
Portrait of Bedfordshire : David H. Kennett : Hale
In Bedfordshire Byways : A. W. Baldwin and W. E. Palmer : Sidney Press
Old Bedfordshire : Simon Houfe : White Crescent Press
Pictorial Guide to Bedfordshire : Eric Meadows : White Crescent Press
History of Bedfordshire : Joyce Godber : Beds County Council
Bedfordshire Mills : Hugh Howes : Beds County Council
Lovely Britain : S. P. B. Mais and Tom Stephenson : Odhams
English Cottages : Tony Evans and Candida Lycett-Green : Weidenfeld & Nicolson
Bedford in Times Past : A. E. Baker and N. C. Wilde : Countryside Publications

CLOPHILL CHURCH

PLACES OPEN TO THE PUBLIC

NGS: National Gardens Scheme   NT: National Trust

AMPTHILL	Avenue House, collection of the late Sir Albert Richardson (by appointment)
	Ampthill Park.
ASPLEY GUISE	Aspley House Gardens (NGS).
	Manor Close Gardens (NGS).
BEDFORD	Bedford Museum (daily except Monday, Christmas and Good Friday).
	Bunyan Museum and Library, Mill Street (weekdays).
	Cecil Higgins Museum, Castle Close (daily except Christmas and Good Friday).
CARDINGTON	Howard's House Gardens (NGS).
DUNSTABLE	The Downs (NT).
ELSTOW	Moot Hall Bunyan Museum (Tuesday to Sunday).
EVERTON	Woodbury Hall Gardens (NGS).
FELMERSHAM	Nature Reserve.
HINWICK	Hinwick House (Easter Monday, Spring and Summer Holiday Mondays and by appointment).
HOUGHTON CONQUEST	Houghton House (NT).
LUTON	Luton Hoo, Wernher Collection and Gardens (Easter to end September, Sunday, Monday, Wednesday, Thursday, Saturday and Good Friday).
	Luton Museum and Art Gallery, Wardown Park.
MAULDEN	Maulden Grange Gardens (NGS).
OAKLEY	Westfields Gardens (NGS).
ODELL	Castle Gardens (NGS) Country Park.
OLD WARDEN	Shuttleworth Aircraft and Transport Museum (daily except Christmas, special flying days in summer).
SANDY	Sandy Lodge RSPB (April–September on Monday to Saturday, October–March on Monday to Friday).
SHARPENHOE	Clappers (NT).
SILSOE	Wrest Park Gardens (April – early October, weekends and Bank Holidays).
SOUTHILL	Southill Park Gardens (NGS).
STAGSDEN	Bird Gardens (except Christmas Day).
STEVINGTON	Post-mill.
STOCKGROVE	Country Park.
SUNDON	Country Park.
TOTTERNHOE	Knolls Nature Reserve.
WHIPSNADE	Zoo (except Christmas Day).
WOBURN	Abbey and Wild Animal Kingdom (all year, daily).

INDEX

Numbers in italics indicate illustrations

Books Published by THE BOOK CASTLE

JOURNEYS INTO HERTFORDSHIRE: Anthony Mackay. Foreword by The Marquess of Salisbury, Hatfield House. Nearly 200 superbly detailed ink drawings depict the towns, buildings and landscape of this still predominantly rural county.

JOURNEYS INTO BEDFORDSHIRE: Anthony Mackay. Foreword by The Marquess of Tavistock, Woburn Abbey. A lavish book of over 150 evocative ink drawings.

ARCHAEOLOGY OF THE CHILTERNS: edited by Robin Holgate. The latest research by authoritative experts throughout the area.

NORTH CHILTERNS CAMERA, 1863–1954: From the Thurston Collection in Luton Museum: edited by Stephen Bunker. Rural landscapes, town views, studio pictures and unique royal portraits by the area's leading early photographer.

LEAFING THROUGH LITERATURE: Writers' Lives in Hertfordshire and Bedfordshire: David Carroll. Illustrated short biographies of many famous authors and their connections with these counties.

THROUGH VISITORS' EYES: A Bedfordshire Anthology: edited by Simon Houfe. Impressions of the county by famous visitors over the last four centuries, thematically arranged and illustrated with line drawings.

THE HILL OF THE MARTYR: An Architectural History of St. Albans Abbey: Eileen Roberts. Scholarly and readable chronological narrative history of Hertfordshire and Bedfordshire's famous cathedral. Fully illustrated with photographs and plans.

LOCAL WALKS: South Bedfordshire and North Chilterns: Vaughan Basham. Twenty-seven thematic circular walks.

LOCAL WALKS: North and Mid-Bedfordshire: Vaughan Basham. Twenty-five thematic circular walks.

OXFORDSHIRE WALKS: Oxford, the Cotswolds and the Cherwell Valley: Nick Moon. One of two volumes planned to complement Chiltern Walks: Oxfordshire and complete coverage of the county, in association with the Oxford Fieldpaths Society.

CHILTERN WALKS: Buckinghamshire: Nick Moon.

CHILTERN WALKS: Oxfordshire and West Buckinghamshire: Nick Moon.

CHILTERN WALKS: Hertfordshire, Bedfordshire and North Buckinghamshire: Nick Moon. Part of the trilogy of circular walks, in association with the Chiltern Society. Each volume contains thirty circular walks.

FOLK: Characters and Events in the History of Bedfordshire and Northamptonshire: Vivienne Evans. Anthology about people of yesteryear – arranged alphabetically by village or town.

LEGACIES: Tales and Legends of Luton and the North Chilterns: Vic Lea. Twenty-five mysteries and stories based on fact, including Luton Town Football Club. Many photographs.

ECHOES: Tales and Legends of Bedfordshire and Hertfordshire: Vic Lea. Thirty, compulsively retold historical incidents.

ECCENTRICS and VILLAINS, HAUNTINGS and HEROES. Tales from Four Shires: Northants, Beds, Bucks and Herts: John Houghton. True incidents and curious events covering one thousand years.

THE RAILWAY AGE IN BEDFORDSHIRE: Fred Cockman. Classic, illustrated account of early railway history.

BEDFORDSHIRE'S YESTERYEARS: Vol. 1: The Family, Childhood and Schooldays: Brenda Fraser-Newstead. Unusual early 20th century reminiscences, with private photographs.

BEDFORDSHIRE'S YESTERYEARS: Vol. 2: The Rural Scene: Brenda Fraser-Newstead. Vivid first-hand accounts of country life two or three generations ago.

WHIPSNADE WILD ANIMAL PARK: 'MY AFRICA': Lucy Pendar. Foreword by Andrew Forbes. Introduction by Gerald Durrell. Inside story of sixty years of the Park's animals and people – full of anecdotes, photographs and drawings.

DUNSTABLE WITH THE PRIORY, 1100–1550: Vivienne Evans. Dramatic growth of Henry I's important new town around a major crossroads.

DUNSTABLE DECADE: THE EIGHTIES – A Collection of Photographs: Pat Lovering. A souvenir book of nearly 300 pictures of people and events in the 1980s.

DUNSTABLE IN DETAIL: Nigel Benson. A hundred of the town's buildings and features, plus town trail map.

OLD DUNSTABLE: Bill Twaddle. A new edition of this collection of early photographs.

BOURNE AND BRED: A Dunstable Boyhood Between the Wars: Colin Bourne. An elegantly written, well-illustrated book capturing the spirit of the town over fifty years ago.

ROYAL HOUGHTON: Pat Lovering. Illustrated history of Houghton Regis from earliest times to the present.

THE CHANGING FACE OF LUTON: An Illustrated History: Stephen Bunker, Robin Holgate and Marian Nichols. Luton's development from earliest times to the present busy industrial town. Illustrated in colour and monochrome. The three authors from Luton Museum are all experts in local history, archaeology, crafts and social history.

THE MEN WHO WORE STRAW HELMETS: Policing Luton, 1840-1974: Tom Madigan. Meticulously chronicled history; dozens of rare photographs; author served Luton Police for nearly fifty years.

BETWEEN THE HILLS: The Story of Lilley, a Chiltern Village: Roy Pinnock. A priceless piece of our heritage – the rural beauty remains but the customs and way of life described here have largely disappeared.

FARM OF MY CHILDHOOD, 1925–1947: Mary Roberts. An almost vanished lifestyle on a remote farm near Flitwick.

EVA'S Story: Chesham Since the Turn of the Century: Eva Rance. The ever-changing twentieth-century, especially the early years at her parents' general stores. Tebby's in the High Street.

THE TALL HITCHIN SERGEANT: A Victorian Crime Novel based on fact: Edgar Newman. Mixes real police officers and authentic background with an exciting storyline.

COUNTRY AIR: SUMMER and AUTUMN: Ron Wilson. The Radio Northampton presenter looks month by month at the countryside's wildlife, customs and lore.

COUNTRY AIR: WINTER and SPRING: Ron Wilson. This companion volume completes the year in the countryside.

Specially for Children

VILLA BELOW THE KNOLLS: A Story of Roman Britain: Michael Dundrow. An exciting adventure for young John in Totternhoe and Dunstable two thousand years ago.

ADVENTURE ON THE KNOLLS: A Story of Iron Age Britain: Michael Dundrow. Excitement on Totternhoe Knolls as ten-year-old John finds himself back in those dangerous times, confronting Julius Caesar and his army.

THE RAVENS: One Boy Against the Might of Rome: James Dyer. On the Barton Hills and in the south-east of England as the men of the great fort of Ravensburgh (near Hexton) confront the invaders.

Further titles are in preparation.
All the above are available via any bookshop, or from the publisher and bookseller

THE BOOK CASTLE
12 Church Street, Dunstable, Bedfordshire LU5 4RU.

Tel: (0582) 605670